Introduction

Bright Ideas
Problem Solving

Written by Archie Millar and Jill Bennett

Published by Scholastic Publications Ltd,
Marlborough House, Holly Walk,
Leamington Spa, Warwickshire CV32 6EQ

© 1990 Scholastic Publications Ltd

Written by Archie Millar and Jill Bennett
Edited by Christine Lee
Sub-edited by Anne Faundez
Illustrated by Gay Galsworthy
Artwork by Liz Preece, Castle Graphics,
Kenilworth

Printed in Great Britain by Loxley Brothers
Ltd, Sheffield

British Library Cataloguing in Publication Data
Millar, Archie
   Bright ideas: problem solving.
   1. Primary schools. Students. Cognitive development.
   Teaching methods
   I. Title   II. Bennett, Jill
   370.152

ISBN 0-590-76331-8

Front and back covers designed by Sue Limb

Contents

WHY INCLUDE PROBLEM SOLVING IN THE CURRICULUM?

At a time when the introduction of the National Curriculum is seen, by some, to be a recipe for restricted practices, it is perhaps natural to ask why problem solving should be considered. Problem-solving work can be time-consuming and messy and potentially expensive if not adequately prepared.

Problem solving re-appears across the curriculum in various forms and at times is specifically regarded as an area to be pursued. It can be incorporated into work on language, mathematics, environmental studies, science, technology, aesthetic experience and RE.

As a cross-curricular concept it can have a unifying effect on curricular meaning, breaking down subject barriers and sexual stereotyping as well as providing children with a process by which to cope with 'problems' encountered in life.

Important aspects of the problem-solving process are the encouragement of idea-sharing amongst children, co-operative working and the need to learn from others irrespective of social and cultural differences.

THE ROLE OF THE CHILD

Let us consider what children have to do in pursuing a problem-solving activity. They have to:

- Consider, discuss and define the exact nature of the problem concerned.
- Suggest possible ideas for a solution (this is a kind of brain-storming session, where any available knowledge is brought to bear on the problem).
- Agree on an approach upon which to work.
- Work together on this approach by whatever methods are agreed.
- Test and evaluate results.
- Make any necessary modifications in the light of their findings.

THE ROLE OF THE TEACHER

Essentially the teacher has to:

- Present the problem.
- Prepare any materials required.
- Observe the children at work, intervening only when an impasse is reached. The teacher should not contribute in a way which will resolve the problem for them.
- Talk with the children at the end of the session, asking questions to help them assess their work for themselves.

Questions the teacher could ask at the end of the session might include:

How did you decide on your strategy and materials?

To what extent were your strategy and materials appropriate?

Was there any other material you wanted to use which was not available to you?

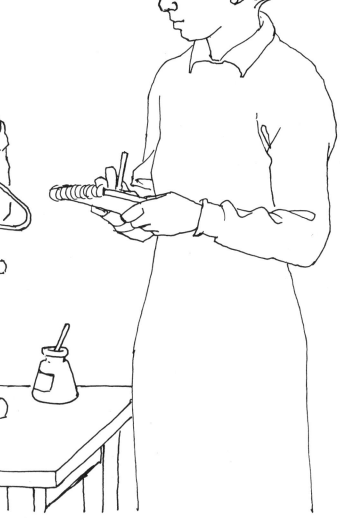

MONITORING PERFORMANCE

When monitoring the children's performance the teacher might ask herself:

- Was the introduction effective without giving answers?
- To what extent was collaborative thinking evident through the quality of comments and suggestions made by the children?
- What use did the children make of drawings and notes in formulating possible solutions?
- Was their interaction effective? Did everyone play a part in offering suggestions and did they listen to each other's ideas?
- How did groups evaluate their solutions?

- Was reference made to the precise nature of the original problem, and what modifications were made to the solutions presented?

MODIFYING PROBLEMS
When using this book, teachers may well be able to modify some of the problems to suit circumstances of immediate practical relevance to their own schools or the community in which they work. If this can be done, all well and good. Problem solving is an essential life-skill which draws on many areas of experience as well as the support and co-operation of others in arriving at a successful conclusion.

Playtime

Children's play is a rich source of problem-solving activities, and the ideas on the following pages are based on play situations where solutions assist the enjoyment and fairness of play. Aspects considered include making toys, inventing games, communicating ideas and working together. The safety aspect is, of course, stressed.

Danger!

Task
Devise a set of rules to illustrate to younger children the dangers of playing near parked cars.

Age range
Nine upwards.

Group size
Small groups.

What you need
Pencils, paper, staplers, felt-tipped pens, crayons, tape recorders and blank tapes.

What to do

Discuss with the children the dangers of playing in and around parked cars.

Ask each group to devise and present a means of communicating these dangers to younger children. The presentation could take the form of drama, a television commercial, a booklet or a cassette story.

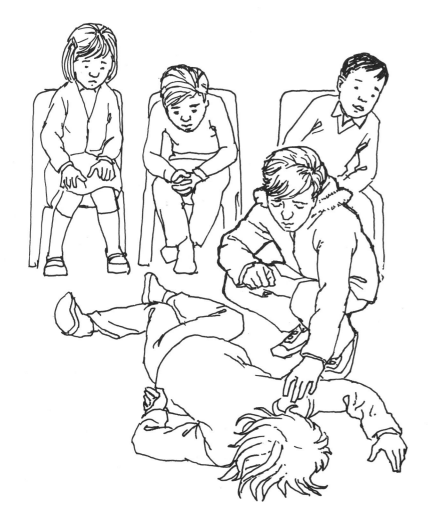

Blowing in the wind

Task
Make a mobile with eight birds for a small child's room.

Age range
Seven upwards.

Group size
Individuals or pairs.

What you need
Thin card, paper in a variety of colours, thin wire, thread, adhesive, scissors, coloured pens, needles or hole punch, thin dowel, straws, any other items the children may request.

What to do
Discuss the purpose of a mobile for a small child.

Ask the children to design and make a mobile according to the task. They will need to decide whether each element of the mobile should be different. They will need to decide how it is to be suspended. For example, they could use a circle of wire to suspend all items or use tiers on a number of rods.

Balancing toy

Task
Make a balancing toy for a small child.

Age range
Seven upwards.

Group size
Individuals or pairs.

What you need
Card of various thicknesses, very thin plywood, adhesives, thin string, scissors, shaper saw or similar, any other items the children may request.

What to do
Discuss the purpose of the toy with the group. What sorts of balancing toys are the children familiar with?

The children should be aware that the finished toy must be colourful but also safe for a young child to play with.

They also need to think about how the toy will balance. For example, it could be on a taut length of thin string, or on a sphere of some kind.

Matching pairs game

Task
Design and make a game (with instructions) which, like dominoes, can be played by matching pairs of blocks or cards but does not depend on counting skills.

Age range
Seven upwards.

Group size
Small groups.

What you need
A set of dominoes, thick card or matchboxes to make blocks, scissors, coloured paper, paint, coloured pens, adhesive, paper, pencils, any other items the children may request.

What to do
Discuss with the children the need to decide on a theme for their domino game. Suggest to them that they study the conventional dominoes set. They need to find out:
- How many dominoes there are;
- How many times each number appears;
- How many times a blank appears.

Ask the children to consider whether their game will need the same proportion of characters or numbers.

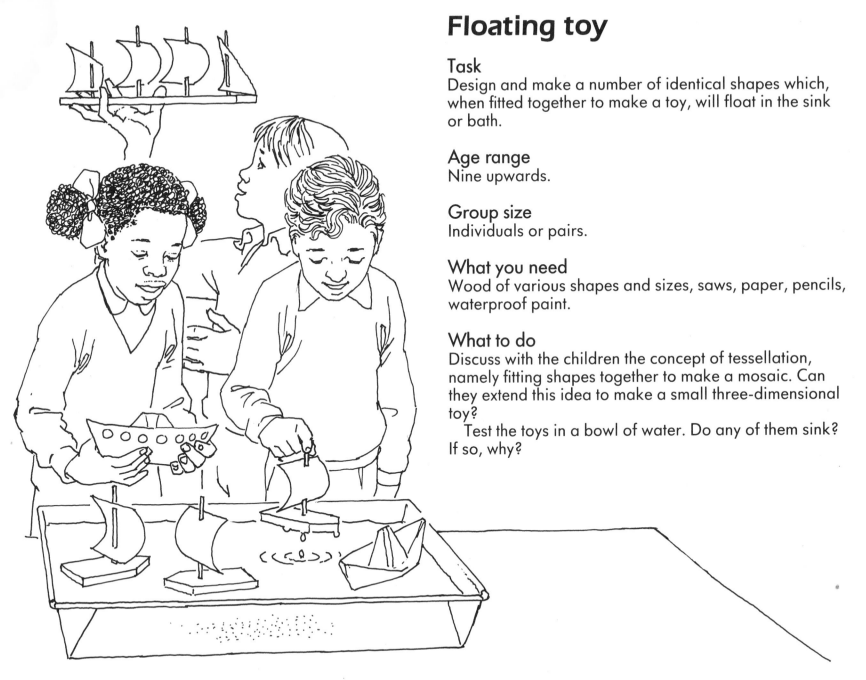

Floating toy

Task
Design and make a number of identical shapes which, when fitted together to make a toy, will float in the sink or bath.

Age range
Nine upwards.

Group size
Individuals or pairs.

What you need
Wood of various shapes and sizes, saws, paper, pencils, waterproof paint.

What to do
Discuss with the children the concept of tessellation, namely fitting shapes together to make a mosaic. Can they extend this idea to make a small three-dimensional toy?

Test the toys in a bowl of water. Do any of them sink? If so, why?

Racket game

Task
Make a set of two rackets and a ball, or shuttlecock, which is safe to use in the classroom. Invent a set of rules for your game.

Age range
Eight upwards.

Group size
Pairs.

What you need
Newspapers, various types of card, adhesive, wire coat-hangers, tissue paper, scissors, dowel, other thin lengths of light wood, elastic bands, art straws, paper clips, string, polythene sheeting, plastic carrier bags, other junk items the children may request.

What to do
Discuss the shape of a basic racket. How will the children's compare? What kind of ball, or shuttle, will they make? How can they modify this to keep it up in the air for longer if necessary? Emphasise the importance of the safety of the game.

The children may well start by trying to make a strung racket. Do not discourage them initially; they will probably discover that it is almost impossible for them to string the racket tight enough without causing the frame to break or distort under the strain. They will then need to consider other alternatives such as using polythene sheeting.

When the children have completed their task, ask them to try out each other's games.

Jigsaw puzzle

Task
Design and make a simple jigsaw puzzle of six to ten pieces depicting a nursery rhyme.

Age range
Seven upwards.

Group size
Individuals or pairs.

What you need
Cardboard of various thicknesses, thin plywood, scissors, shaper saw or similar, paints, paper, felt-tipped pens, adhesive.

What to do
Ask the children to decide on a theme for their picture. Suggest they draw out their designs on paper before transferring it on to the card or wood. If the children choose to make their puzzle from wood, they will need to be able to use a shaper saw or equivalent; if they are unfamiliar with the use of this item, they will need to practise beforehand.

Ask them how and where they should draw out the shape of the pieces. How will they store the jigsaw? Will they need to make a container for the pieces?

Without any words

Task
Design a poster which could be used to show a child who cannot understand English how to play a traditional game, for example hopscotch.

Age range
Seven upwards.

Group size
Individuals or pairs.

What you need
Large sheets of paper, pens, crayons, pencils, paints.

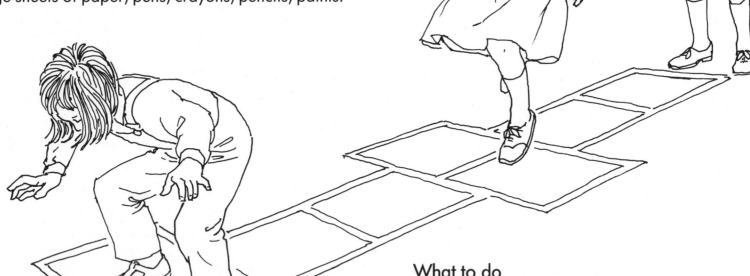

What to do
Discuss with the children the problem of communicating with someone whose language is different from theirs. What are the alternatives to words?

Encourage the children to make rough plans of their sequence before working on the large posters.

Puppets

Task
Make a cardboard puppet representing a character from a traditional story.

Age range
Seven upwards.

Group size
Individuals or pairs.

What you need
Thin card, adhesive, scissors, paper clips, pens, paints and brushes, string, elastic bands.

What to do
Let the children decide on the character to be made. Do they understand the term 'traditional story'?

What will the puppet be like? Do they want the character to have moving limbs? If so, how will this be achieved?

Stress that they should only use card and paper for the puppet, not fabric.

Calculator game

Task
Invent a game for two players using card and pocket calculators.

Age range
Nine upwards.

Group size
Pairs.

What you need
Calculators, paper, pencils, thin card, pens.

What to do
Explain the limitations to the children. They may decide, for example, to make either a subtraction game or an addition game. They may decide to make a set of number cards, with a number to be added or subtracted from their total each time.

Once the pair has perfected the game, they will need to write a set of instructions for other pairs to follow. Let the pairs try out each other's games.

Story board game

Task
Invent a board game based on a story you have enjoyed recently.

Age range
Seven upwards.

Group size
Small groups.

What you need
Paper, pencils, the book on which the game is to be based, card, felt-tipped pens, scissors, other small items the children may request.

What to do
Ask the groups to consider various questions:
- How many players can be involved?
- What will be used for players' pieces?
- Will dice be required? If so, do these need to be made?
- On what basis will the winner be decided: the first to a particular spot? The one with the most cards or tokens?

A set of written rules will need to be formulated. When these have been tested by the group concerned, the game can then be given to another group to try out. Are any modifications needed?

Follow-up
How will the components of the game be stored? Design and make a suitable container which will hold all the parts of the game.

Nursery rhyme book

Task
Make a 'First Nursery Rhyme Book' for a two-year-old child. Include only ten rhymes, each of which must be illustrated.

Age range
Seven upwards.

Group size
Individuals or small groups.

What you need
Collection of nursery rhyme books, paper, coloured paper, pens, paint, crayons, pastels, scissors, adhesive, thick and thin card.

What to do
Ask the children to decide on their ten rhymes. What will they use as the basis for their selection?

What medium will be used for the illustrations? Will each rhyme have the same illustrator? Will each rhyme be on a separate page? How will the book be bound? What size should the pages be? What will the book's title be?

Follow-up
Make a pop-up book for a small child using the text of a nursery rhyme from the 'First Nursery Rhyme Book'.

Blindfold game

Task
Invent a game for four players where all the players are blindfolded.

Age range
Nine upwards.

Group size
Fours.

What you need
Paper, blindfolds. Other items will depend on the kind of game invented, but could include food items or objects with different textures.

What to do
Discuss with the children the difficulties posed by being unable to see. When devising their game they will need to bear in mind the safety element. Should the game be played sitting down? If not, what safety precautions need to be taken?

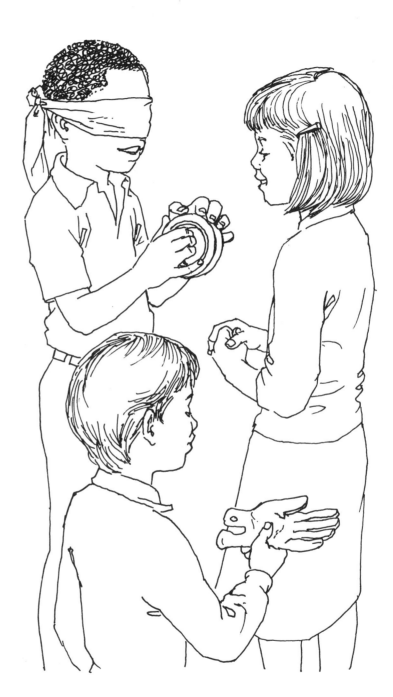

Alphabet book

Task
Design and make an alphabet book for a young child on one of the following themes: animals, things to eat, or everyday things in the home and garden.

Age range
Seven upwards.

Group size
Small groups.

What you need
Paper, pencils, pens, crayons, paints, thin card.

What to do
Once the children have chosen their theme, they will need to make an alphabetical list of items to be illustrated. Will both lower-case letters and capitals be used? If not, which will they choose and why? What will the book be called?

Story-book ingredients

Task
Invent a fantasy story to be made into a picture book based on the following items: a teapot with a willow pattern design (or similar); a soup plate of alphabet noodles; a salt cellar; a pepper pot; a spoon; a cup and saucer; a bowl of fruit.

Age range
Eight upwards.

Group size
Pairs.

What you need
A collection of the items listed above if possible, paper, pens, crayons, paints, pastels.

What to do
Present the children with the task. Have a table set with the items listed. Give the children plenty of time to discuss their ideas. What characters will they include?

With older children you may like to discuss how picture books are made up. The number of pages is normally a multiple of eight: eight pages, 16 pages, 24 pages, 32 pages and so on. Make the page numbers an additional element of the task.

Radio magazine show

Task
Make a five minute tape for a children's radio magazine show. Include several items rather than one long one.

Age range
Nine upwards.

Group size
Small groups.

What you need
Paper, pencils, tape recorders, blank tapes, timers, any other items the children may request.

What to do
Present the task to the children, reminding them that a number of items are required. These might be jokes, short stories, songs, poems, book reviews, quizzes etc, but try to let them suggest their own items.

As well as deciding upon what should be included, the children will need to think about the following points:
- In what order will the items be?
- Will each item be introduced? If so, how?
- Will there be any sound effects?
- At what age group are they targeting their programme?

Land yachts

Task
Using only LEGO and paper sails, design and make a
land yacht which can be blown along by moving a sheet
of thin card.

Age range
Seven upwards.

Group size
Individuals or small groups.

What you need
LEGO, paper, scissors, felt-tipped pens, card.

What to do
Present the problem to the children. Ensure that they
understand what is meant by a 'land yacht'.

Let the children race their models. Whose is fastest?
Why? When racing their models they will need to look at
both the design of the craft and the shape and size of
the propelling card. Does the card need to be
standardised to make the race fair?

See-saw

'See-Saw, Marjory Daw,
Johnny shall have a new master,
He shall have but a penny a day
Because he won't work any faster.'

Task
Design and make a working see-saw.

Age range
Seven upwards.

Group size
Pairs or small groups.

What you need
Cardboard, wood offcuts, hack-saws, adhesive, screws or nails, screwdriver, any other items the children may suggest.

What to do
Read the rhyme to the class, then present them with the task. They will need to find the balancing point of the see-saw and a way of attaching it to the fulcrum yet leaving it to pivot freely.

Blowing bubbles

Task
How many different bubble-blowing devices can you design and make?

Age range
Seven upwards.

Group size
Pairs or small groups.

What you need
Drinking straws, elastic bands, string, wire coat-hangers, flexible wire, polystyrene cups, scissors, wire cutters, fairly large shallow tray for bubble solution, bubble solution: 300 ml water, 85 ml washing-up liquid, 15 ml glycerine, two teaspoons sugar.

What to do
Present the children with the task. You may wish to supply the bubble solution ready made up or let its preparation be part of the task.

Follow-up
When the children have completed their designs they could think about the following problems:
- Try to make the biggest bubble you can. Which device is best for this?
- Can bubbles be made in single colours?
- Can you find a surface off which bubbles will bounce without breaking? Investigate wood, cloth, grass, linoleum etc.

Bouncy ball

Task
Find out from what height a tennis ball must be dropped so that it bounces to a height of 25 centimetres.

Age range
Seven upwards.

Group size
Small groups.

What you need
Tennis balls, metre rules, paper, pencils, pens, elastic bands.

What to do
Make sure the children understand that the ball is to be dropped, not bounced, at the start of the test. How will they record their findings?

Score board

Task
Design and make a simple, clearly legible score board for either a quiz game or a sports event.

Age range
Nine upwards.

Group size
Small groups.

What you need
Paper, card, drawing materials, scissors, adhesive tape.

What to do
Discuss the presentation of scores in quiz games and sporting events. The children will be familiar with many scoring games from television programmes. Sometimes the score may take the form of a time taken or a distance travelled. Which are the children's favourite methods?

Ask the children to devise a simple system to display scores, which is clearly visible from a distance, easily changed (as scores or competitors change) and gives the information accurately. They will also need to investigate the visibility factor of various colour combinations.

Can they devise a game which would be appropriate to their score board?

Fairground ride

Task
Design and make a working model of an exciting ride for a fairground.

Age range
Seven upwards.

Group size
Small groups.

What you need
Cardboard, dowelling, tubes, adhesive tape, cotton reels, elastic bands, scissors, paper clips, adhesives, any other items the children may request.

What to do
Discuss the task with the children and ask them to imagine that they are fairground designers. They will first have to decide upon the ride to be made.

They will then need to think about various factors:
- How will it stand up?
- Will it need to revolve? If so, how?
- How many seats will it contain?
- Do they want to control the speed of the ride? If so, how might this be done?

The children may wish to design the model to accommodate small figures such as LEGO men, or dolls. If so, they will need to relate the size of their model to the figures used. What safety precautions will they need to think about and incorporate into the design?

Rocking chair

Task
Design and make a rocking chair for a doll or teddy bear.

Age range
Seven upwards.

Group size
Small groups.

What you need
Cardboard, adhesives, adhesive tape, scissors, small boxes, paper, pencils, any other items the children may suggest, a selection of soft toys and dolls.

What to do
Discuss with the children the movement made by a rocking chair; you may wish to link this with a PE session. What shapes help create a rocking movement?

Obviously the children will need to think about their design in relation to the soft toy but it may be useful for them first to draw some ideas.

At school

In this chapter situations relevant to schools and their organisations are explored to enable the children to examine issues and devise practical solutions to them. All the ideas offered will help enhance the children's appreciation of how a school is run.

Clearly, there are many ideas which are more specific to certain schools than others, and the sheer geography of individual sites might suggest communication and logistical issues for further development. The children could be allowed to modify ideas in accordance with their own school's requirements.

Sight aid

Task
Devise a means of helping someone with poor sight to find the way from the classroom to the headteacher's office.

Age range
Nine upwards.

Group size
Small groups or pairs.

What you need
Blindfolds, string, carpet offcuts, sandpaper, polystyrene pieces, any other materials the children may suggest.

What to do
Discuss the importance of good eyesight and the difficulties of living without it. A simple blindfold game could illustrate this.

Ask the children to devise a system to assist someone with poor eyesight to find the way to the headteacher's office.

The children may try to make some kind of tactile trail. Clearly it must not put the user or any others in the school in danger. Discuss with the children the use of pimpled paving stones at pedestrian crossings.

Fire drill instructions

Task
There is to be a fire drill at school. Devise the best way for the children to leave the classroom and proceed to the playground in a quick but orderly way. Write out the instructions.

Age range
Nine upwards.

Group size
Small groups.

What you need
Paper, pencils.

What to do
Present the task to the children. Obviously it will be of great value if each group can test out its instructions on the rest of the class. The class could then decide which set of instructions works best.

Book case

Task
Design and make a container which will hold and protect a paperback book in transit from school to home and back.

Age range
Seven upwards.

Group size
Pairs.

What you need
Card or stiff paper, scissors, adhesives, adhesive tape, masking tape, stapler, a selection of paperbacks.

What to do
Discuss with the children the importance of carrying paperback books safely to and from school. Point out how easily they can get damaged if they are just thrown into a sports bag or carrier.

Let the children design and make a container which will encase and protect a paperback in transit from school to home and back. It should also protect it from spilled drinks, younger children and pets at home.

Book cover

Task
Design and make a cover to help preserve a paperback book. It must be easily removable.

Age range
Seven upwards.

Group size
Pairs or groups of three.

What you need
Paperback books, sheets of paper at least A3 size, string, adhesive tape, scissors, elastic bands, adhesives.

What to do
Make available a range of paperbacks, some with spines, some without. Let the children look at different kinds of books before setting them the task.

The children can discuss whether the cover should have any form of decoration on it. If so, what would be appropriate, bearing in mind that the cover may be transferred from one book to another? Obviously the kind of book selected by the group will have a bearing on the design of the cover.

Book display

Task
Design, make and test a stand to display a book no bigger than 25 cm × 27 cm.

Age range
Eight upwards.

Group size
Pairs or small groups.

What you need
Wood offcuts, wire, adhesives, wire coat-hangers, nails, hammers, books, any other items the children may suggest.

What to do
Discuss the ways in which books are displayed.

What features of the book need to be visible? How can the display stand be made stable?

Arrange a visit to a public library or bookshop so that the children can see different ways in which books can be displayed.

Book tidy

Task
Design and make a device which can be used to hold a set of up to six paperback books.

Age range
Eight upwards.

Group size
Small groups.

What you need
Paperback books, cardboard, adhesives, scissors, pens, staples, any other items the children may suggest.

What to do
Discuss with the children the problem of sets of paperbacks (for instance, *The Chronicles of Narnia*) being split up on the classroom shelves and possibly becoming dog-eared. How can this be prevented?

Let groups of children design and make their own cases, or holders, for sets of books. Let the class decide which are the most effective and use them in the class library.

Back to the classroom

Task
Devise a system for reducing the time lost when children come in from the playground at the end of playtime.

Age range
Nine upwards.

Group size
Small groups.

What you need
Paper, pencils.

What to do
Discuss with the children the problem concerning the amount of time lost when they come in from the playground. You might also like to suggest that groups should observe what actually happens at the end of one or two playtimes.

Ask each group to devise a means of reducing this lost time but still bringing the children in sensibly and safely.

Let each group present its solution in a report-back session and encourage the rest of the class to ask questions.

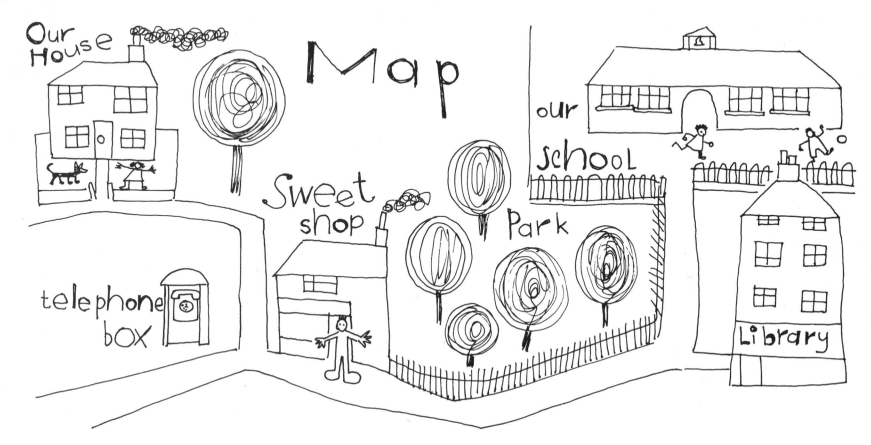

Finding the way

Task
Make a map showing the route to your home from school.

Age range
Seven upwards.

Group size
Individuals.

What you need
Paper, pencils, drawing materials.

What to do
Tell the children that some friends are coming home with them for tea after school. None of them has ever been to the house before, so a map is needed to help them find their way using the school as a starting point. Important markers such as a telephone kiosk, post box or shops should be shown.

The map could be part of an invitation designed by the children on the theme of 'explorer's tea time'.

Our school booklet

Task
Produce a booklet for new children telling them about your school and its immediate surroundings.

Age range
Seven upwards.

Group size
Small groups.

What you need
Paper, pencils, drawing materials, cameras, film, tape recorders and blank tapes.

What to do
Discuss with the children the problems encountered by new families moving into the area.

Ask the children to think of places of interest in the community and to produce a booklet for children who are new to the school, which will tell them about the area. Ask them to include illustrated information about the school.

Alternatively, let groups produce a picture book with an accompanying tape giving the information.

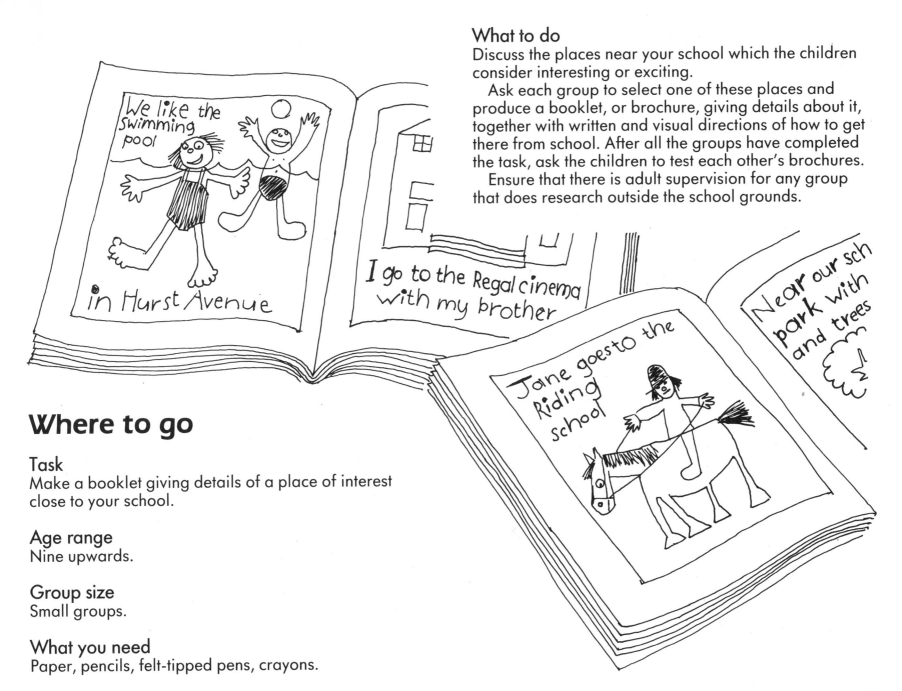

What to do

Discuss the places near your school which the children consider interesting or exciting.

Ask each group to select one of these places and produce a booklet, or brochure, giving details about it, together with written and visual directions of how to get there from school. After all the groups have completed the task, ask the children to test each other's brochures.

Ensure that there is adult supervision for any group that does research outside the school grounds.

Where to go

Task
Make a booklet giving details of a place of interest close to your school.

Age range
Nine upwards.

Group size
Small groups.

What you need
Paper, pencils, felt-tipped pens, crayons.

Text within the illustration:
We like the swimming pool in Hurst Avenue

I go to the Regal cinema with my brother

Jane goes to the Riding school

Near our sch[ool] park with and trees

Danger at school

Task
Identify the potential danger areas in your school grounds; make a list of them in order of priority and then present suggestions as to how the dangers might be overcome.

Age range
Nine upwards.

Group size
Small groups.

What you need
Paper, pencils, drawing materials, clipboards.

What to do
Discuss the school site with the children to identify potentially dangerous areas and aspects.

Let the children walk round the school playground during playtime, making notes. Next, organise an inspection of various parts of the building during working time. When each group has made a list, ask the children to put in order of priority the danger areas using criteria arrived at through their own discussions.

Ask them to consider ways in which each danger could be obviated and to present the solution they consider would be most effective. Lists of final solutions could be reported back at a whole-class forum.

Signs of the times

Task
Design and make four signs which are vital for the safety of people in your school.

Age range
Seven upwards.

Group size
Small groups.

What you need
Paper, drawing materials.

What to do
Discuss the provision of signs as a means of conveying important information, for instance road signs, clothes care symbols etc.

The children then need to discuss and decide upon the four main dangers to safety in their school, before discussing how the information might best be conveyed visually. Will they use pictures, symbols, words or a combination of these? Will the messages be in positive or negative terms?

In addition, they need to think about size and shape, and how and where the signs will be displayed.

Draw up the rules

Task
Produce a strip cartoon or other pictorial representation of the school's rules for a poster.

Age range
Seven upwards.

Group size
Small groups.

What you need
Paper, drawing materials.

What to do
Discuss the school rules with the children. Why do they exist and why are they important?

Then let the children decide how each rule can be represented most effectively and incorporate their ideas into a poster.

Day trip

Task
Plan a day trip from school for a class of younger children.

Age range
Nine upwards.

Group size
Small groups.

What you need
Paper, pencils, drawing materials.

What to do
Discuss the possibility of a day visit from school to a place of known interest, approximately ten miles away.

Ask the children to plan the trip for a class (or year group) of younger children. This should include the costing, admission arrangements, letters to parents and so on. They will also need to consider the supervision of the children, arrangements for lunchtime and playtime and decide on clothing suitable for the occasion.

When finding out about costs for transport, entry fees etc, the children may feel it necessary to make telephone calls. You will need to decide whether any such calls should be made through the school secretary or by a member of the class. In either case, the person making the call will need all the relevant information to hand (numbers involved, date, time, length of visit etc).

Pet at large

Task
The class pet has escaped. Design and make a trap which will catch but not hurt it.

Age range
Nine upwards.

Group size
Small groups.

What you need
Wood, hack-saws, hammers, drill, screwdriver, wire, staples, wire mesh, cardboard, adhesives, any other items the children may suggest.

What to do
Discuss the safety aspect with the class, as this is very important. What precautions should they take to ensure that an animal would not be hurt by their device? They will need to decide what particular animal the trap is designed for, as this will have a bearing on its shape and size. How can the trap be tested without using a live animal?

Interview

Task
One of your class is to be on the interview panel for a new school caretaker. Formulate ten questions you think should be asked at the interview.

Age range
Nine upwards.

Group size
Small groups.

What you need
Paper, pencils, clipboards.

What to do
Draft a job description and let the children study it. They will obviously need to think about what the job involves.

Divide the class into small groups and set them the task. At the end of a set time, ask each group to report back to the whole class. Draw up a final list of the most appropriate ten questions.

Extend the task to interview for:
- A new teacher;
- A secretary;
- A dinner supervisor.

Pack-away lunch holder

Task
Design and make a packed-lunch container, which can also be used as a place-mat and then be folded away to take home.

Age range
Seven upwards.

Group size
Pairs.

What you need
Thin cardboard in various sizes, scissors, paper-fasteners, items from a packed lunch or something to represent them, eg a drink carton or a yoghurt pot, pencils, stapler, assorted, empty take-away cartons, manufactured lunch boxes.

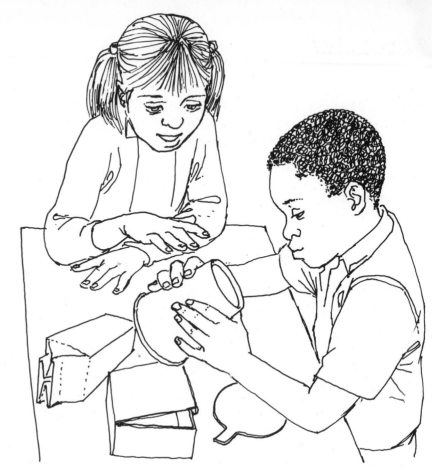

What to do
If possible, have available a range of take-away cartons and lunch boxes for the children to examine. Draw their attention to different features of the containers, such as the material used, base shape and net (if any).

Do any features of the cartons examined prevent their design being used as a model for the task? Do any have features which could be incorporated into the task design? Working from their observations, the children can then create their own designs.

Stop thief!

Task
There has been an outbreak of packed lunches being stolen from your classroom. Devise ways in which you could try to stop this from happening.

Age range
Seven upwards.

Group size
Small groups.

What you need
Paper, pencils, anything else the children may suggest following their discussions.

What to do
Present the children with the task. They should discuss this in their groups and draw up a list of possibilities. Solutions may not involve making a particular item, but, rather, following a course of action.

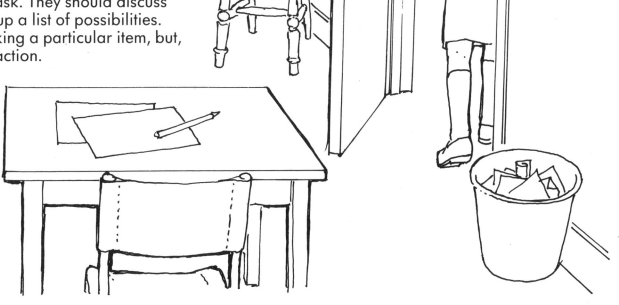

Library jingle

Task
Invent a jingle of no more than 15 words asking people to keep the school library tidy. Create an accompaniment using a beater, maracas, or woodblocks.

Age range
Seven upwards.

Group size
Pairs or small groups.

What you need
Paper, pencils, maracas, wood blocks, beaters, tape recorder and blank tape.

What to do
Set the children the task above.

Ask the class to vote on the best jingles. Make a tape recording of them and base a school assembly around them.

Losing your way

Task
Invent a system for finding the way into an unknown area and out again.

Age range
Nine upwards.

Group size
Individuals.

What you need
A copy of Kenneth Grahame's *Wind in the Willows*, pencils, paper.

What to do
Read the passage from *Wind in the Willows* in which Rat and Mole are lost in the Wild Wood.

Ask the children to devise a system for making a trail into an unknown area (either woodland or built-up suburbia) which they could also use to find their way out. Stress that they have no materials at the outset, only those they can improvise from their surroundings.

Discuss other stories where trails are laid such as Theseus and the Minotaur or Hansel and Gretel.

Storage symbols

Task
Design and produce a series of symbols for identifying the storage areas of resources in the classroom.

Age range
Nine upwards.

Group size
Small groups.

What you need
Paper, drawing materials.

What to do
Discuss the importance of symbols which describe the contents of dangerous areas and the hazards associated with them. Discuss examples such as signs indicating radioactive materials or high voltage.

Ask the children to design symbols to designate the contents of cupboards and other containers in the classroom. The symbols must have no words and must be universally understood.

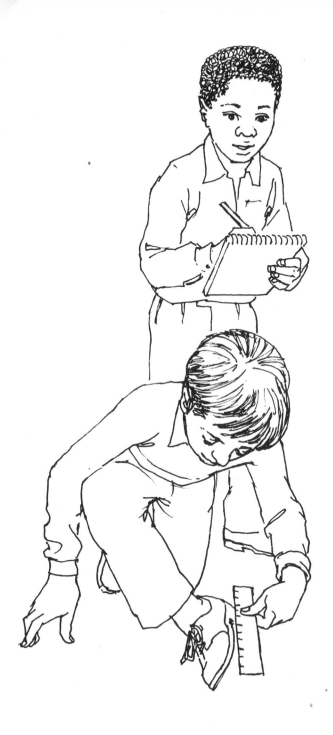

Shoe measure

Task
Design and make something which can be used to measure the shoe size of everyone in your school.

Age range
Seven upwards.

Group size
Small groups.

What you need
Paper, pencils, pens, rulers, wood, cardboard, adhesive tape, adhesives, scissors, any other items the children may suggest.

What to do
Discuss with the children what is meant by shoe size. Are all makes the same as far as sizes are concerned? How long is each size? What is the range of sizes the children need to encompass? How will they obtain the information? Will width be included? If so, how will this be measured?

Ask the children to draw up a table of their findings.

Paper filing cabinet

Task
Using only the materials provided, make a filing cabinet, or similar construction, suitable for storing A4-size paper.

Age range
Nine upwards.

Group size
Small groups.

What you need
Paper, pencils, cardboard, boxes, adhesive, staplers, rulers, scissors.

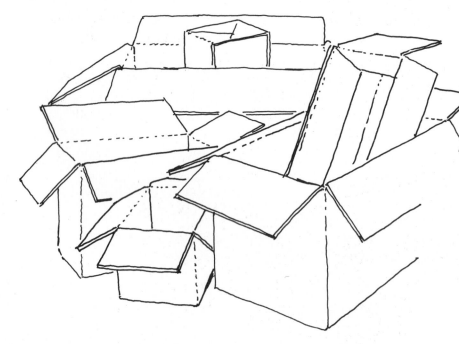

What to do
Present the problem to the children. You may want to let them look at some examples of filing trays before they start their own designs. What do they need to consider in terms of shape and size? Will their design include more than one separate compartment? How can it be made stable? Will it be designed to stand on the floor or on a desk top?

Let the children decide which is the best design and use it in the classroom.

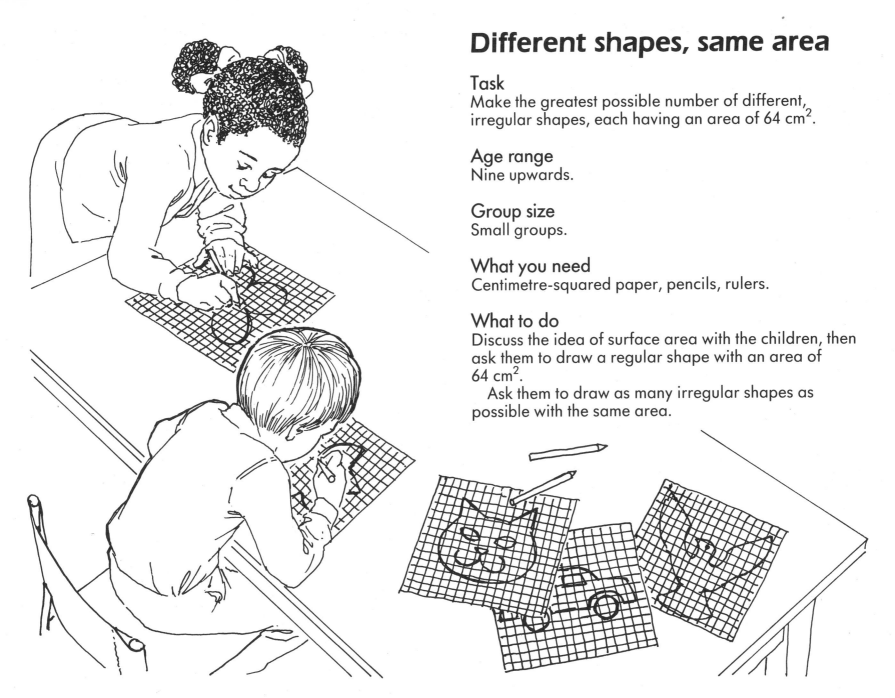

Different shapes, same area

Task
Make the greatest possible number of different, irregular shapes, each having an area of 64 cm^2.

Age range
Nine upwards.

Group size
Small groups.

What you need
Centimetre-squared paper, pencils, rulers.

What to do
Discuss the idea of surface area with the children, then ask them to draw a regular shape with an area of 64 cm^2.

Ask them to draw as many irregular shapes as possible with the same area.

Burglar alarm

Task
Design and make a system which will raise the alarm for the caretaker if your school is broken into.

Age range
Nine upwards.

Group size
Small groups.

What you need
Paper, pencils, batteries, buzzers, bulbholders, plastic-coated copper wire, wire coat-hangers, wire cutters, adhesive tape, wood, nails, hack-saws, hammers, crocodile clips (usually already fixed to wire).

What to do

Discuss with the class the inconvenience of school break-ins to children and teachers. The children then have to devise a system which would raise the alarm for the caretaker and which would also be public enough to warn others.

The important element here is the triggering device. Where should it be put? How will it be activated? What will the alarm signal be?

Good or bad?

Task
Produce a rating scale applicable to the different types of behaviour which are found among children at school.

Age range
Nine upwards.

Group size
Small groups.

What you need
Paper, pencils.

What to do
Discuss the variations of behaviour within the school and ask the children to compile a list of ten to fifteen different types of behaviour. This could include, for example:
- Politeness;
- Swearing;
- Working hard;
- Bullying.

Ask the children to grade these in order of 'best' to 'worst' and allocate each one a number or code (for example, one to ten) to indicate the importance or seriousness of the mode of behaviour in the eyes of the children.

This will necessitate a great deal of discussion within the groups. It would be interesting for the children to note and discuss the priorities of the different groups.

Follow-up

Ask the children to devise a system of sanctions and rewards appropriate to the various types of behaviour. Where appropriate, ask the children to develop these into a code of conduct for the class or school.

At home

There are many aspects of living at home which lend themselves to problem-solving approaches. If only someone would invent a device to clean up a child's bedroom or clear the dining table and wash and stack the dishes!

As with schools, individual circumstances might well reveal specific problems which could be shared with others in the search for a solution. Some of the problems suggested here will prove familiar to the children, while others will require them to use a little imagination.

Bird feeder

Task
Make a container which will hold flat slices of bread and toast to feed the birds.

Age range
Nine upwards.

Group size
Small groups.

What you need
Wire mesh, netting, adhesives, paper, pencils, string, scissors, flexible wire, wood, hack-saws.

What to do
Discuss the idea of throwing out bread and dried toast for the birds. It often lies on the ground and therefore attracts other animals.

Ask the children to devise a container which holds flat slices of bread out of the reach of other animals. This could be a hanging device; or it could be lifted from the ground by a pole or similar means.

Discuss the designs with the whole class. Let the children choose the best designs and build a bird feeder for the school garden.

Remember to avoid feeding unnatural foods during the birds' breeding season – from April to October – as birds should be rearing their young on natural, protein-rich insect food.

Supermarket holdall

Task
Design, make and test a container which will hold eight supermarket items including two cans of beans, a packet of cereal, two packets of tea, a piece of cheese weighing about 250 g and two packets of biscuits. Using the container, you must be able to carry the items from your classroom to another room about 50 metres away.

Age range
Seven upwards.

Group size
Small groups.

What you need
A variety of manufactured carrier bags, large sheets of paper at least A1 size, scissors, a variety of adhesives, adhesive tape, masking tape, string, split pins, stapler, food items from the above list.

Keep it cold

Task
Devise packaging which will keep ice-cream cold for the longest possible time.

Age range
Seven upwards.

Group size
Pairs or small groups.

What you need
A selection of packaging materials such as polystyrene chips, bubble wrap, expanded polystyrene sheets, wool, cardboard, newspaper and padded envelopes; adhesive, adhesive tape, scissors, timers, ice-cubes.

What to do
Let the children examine and dismantle as many different kinds of carrier bags as possible. Their attention can be drawn to features such as handles, bases and shape. Suggest they make a note of any important observations.

Following their investigations, groups can then proceed with the design task. They will need to think especially about what kind of adhesive to use, how the handles are to be made (fixed on to the bag or cut out from it) and whether the bag needs reinforcement anywhere.

What to do

Discuss with the children the problem of bringing ice-cream home from the shop on a hot day; what happens to it? What could they do to stop this from happening?

Experiment with different insulating materials, using ice-cubes to represent ice-cream.

Are some materials better insulators than others?

You may like to introduce this activity by reading a story such as *Ice Creams for Rosie* by Ronda and David Armitage (Hippo Books) or the 'Ice Cream' story from Arnold Lobel's *Frog and Toad All Year* (Heinemann, *I Can Read* series).

Sharing strategies

Task
Your little brother has taken one of your toys, but you want to play with it. If you become angry with him he will probably cry. What will you do?

Age range
Seven upwards.

Group size
Individuals or pairs.

What you need
Pencils, paper.

What to do
Present the children with the task as given. This is a situation they may well be familiar with, so encourage plenty of discussion.

Draw up a diagram to illustrate how different ways of responding could affect the situation. The diagrams could be presented either all in words or in pictorial form.

Photo holder

Task
Make something which can be used to display six photographs, each measuring 10 cm × 15 cm. You should be able to pack it flat so that it can be stored in an envelope or carried in a pocket.

Age range
Nine upwards.

Group size
Pairs.

What you need
Card of different sizes including A4 and A1, adhesive tape, string, pipe-cleaners, paper clips, elastic bands, photographs, scissors.

What to do
Present the children with the problem. There are several ways of tackling it; some depend on the size of card selected. Essentially, the children are likely to follow one of two lines of thought: either to make individual frames for each photo and then make up a stand or to make a concertina-type stand, or even a cuboid. The second solution is perhaps more likely if a large piece of card has been selected. Some children, however, may be able to make a concertina effect by taping small pieces of card edge to edge.

They will need to consider problems such as how to get the photos to stay in the stand and whether more than one photo will fit on one side of a concertina arrangement.

Milk indicator

Task
Design and make a device for letting the person who delivers the milk know how many pints to leave.

Age range
Seven upwards.

Group size
Pairs.

What you need
Wood, card, adhesive, paints, plastic offcuts, paper-fasteners, scissors, hack-saws, empty milk bottles.

What to do
Discuss with the children how notes stuck in milk bottles often get blown away or are made illegible by the rain. Ask them to make an easy-to-read, easy-to-use alternative.

Discuss the different ideas with the class. Try out some of the devices on a rainy day and leave them outside for half a day. Which remain legible?

Keep off!

Task
Devise a means of deterring birds from certain areas of the garden without causing them any physical harm.

Age range
Eight upwards.

Group size
Small groups.

What you need
String, wood offcuts, wire mesh, small plastic pots, milk tops, cardboard, adhesives, any other materials the children may suggest.

What to do
Discuss the fact that there are areas from which people wish to discourage birds. What might these areas be? How could the birds be deterred?

The deterrent could take the form of a physical barrier or it could be a bird scarer of some sort. Do the children know what might frighten birds away?

Home help

Task
Design and make a device which will help an elderly or disabled person to open a book or newspaper, or an object with which to open drawers and cupboard doors.

Age range
Nine upwards.

Group size
Small groups or pairs.

What you need
Wood offcuts, plastic offcuts, hack-saws, adhesives, staplers, coat-hangers, hooks, string, elastic bands, jubilee clips, any other items the children may suggest.

What to do
Discuss the problems of physical handicap, especially those impeding the use of arms and hands. Alternatively, suggest the children talk with elderly people to find out the kinds of problems they have with everyday tasks such as those mentioned above.

After discussion, let the children make their own tools to help solve specific problems.

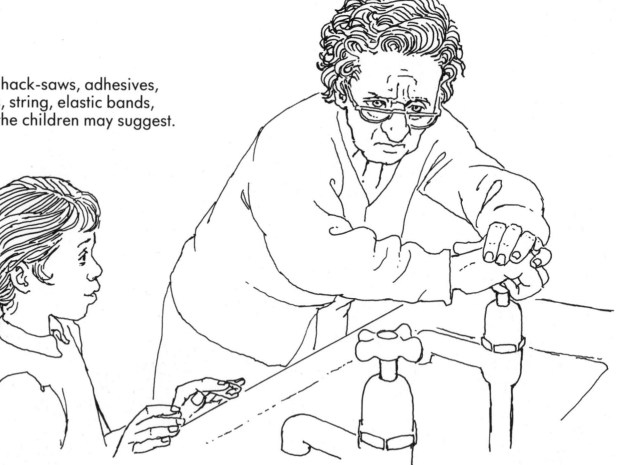

Dog exercise

Task
Devise a system for exercising a dog in an unfenced area.

Age range
Nine upwards.

Group size
Small groups.

What you need
Paper and drawing materials, string, wire.

What to do
Discuss the problems that are likely to occur when exercising a dog in an open area such as a garden which is largely grassed, with a few trees and no solid fencing.

Ask the children to devise a simple system whereby the dog can be confined to the garden without injuring itself if it tries to escape.

The children should present the solution in the form of diagrams with explanatory text before they proceed to the making or testing stage.

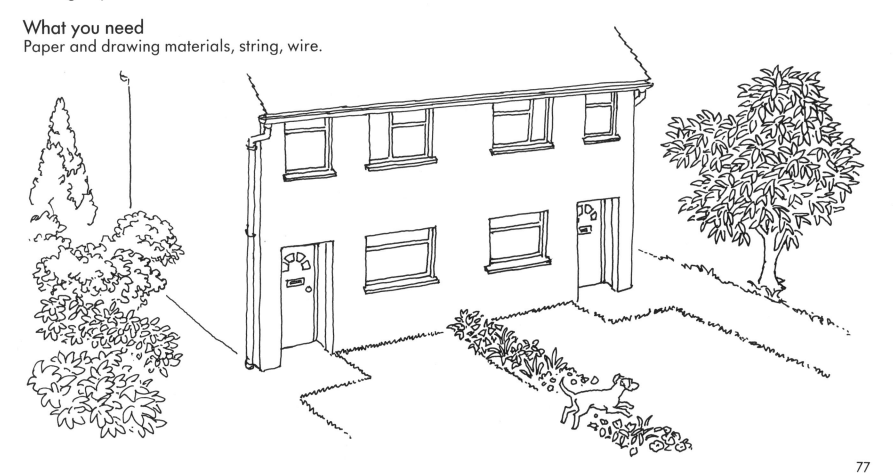

Cooking the lunch

Task

You are going to have a lunch-time snack. Eggs are to be used as the main item and as few extra ingredients as possible are to be added. You cannot use a frying pan or an oven, only a hot plate or a gas ring, and a saucepan. How many different ways can you prepare the eggs?

Age range
Nine upwards.

Group size
Pairs.

What you need
Pencils, paper, card, scissors, pens.

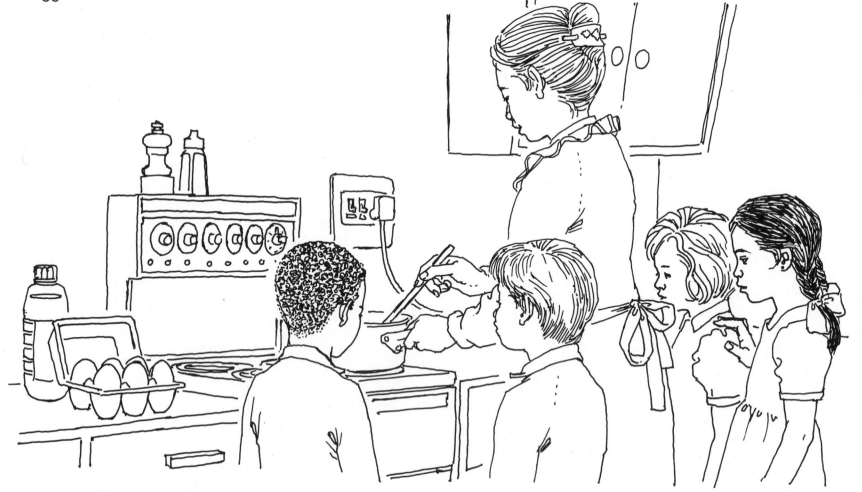

What to do

Present the task to the children. Ask them to consider the following points:

- What ways do they know of preparing eggs?
- Which ways fit in with the requirements given in the task?
- How and where can they find more recipes for preparing eggs?

Ask them to present their ideas in the form of recipe cards, listing ingredients and the method of preparation.

Recipe cards using a strip-cartoon form of illustration could be devised.

Mixed bag

This chapter contains a variety of problem-solving exercises which can be used simply as one-off exercises to develop the problem-solving process. Many of the activities suggested here make use of photocopiable pages which individuals or groups of children can use to record the results of their attempts to solve a given problem.

The activities include practical problems relevant to the children's own experiences as well as ideas using traditional rhymes and fantasy subjects with a more imaginative slant.

Who likes what?

Task
Devise and demonstrate a system which shows the preferences different bird species have for different foods.

Age range
Nine upwards.

Group size
Small groups.

What you need
Bird identification books, wood, hammer, nails, hacksaws, string, small plastic pots, adhesives, paper, pencils.

What to do

Discuss the variety of bird life to be seen around the school and in gardens. Do different species of birds like the same foods?

Ask the children to devise a feeding tray which will hold different foods, then organise a means for recording the preferences of the birds.

The Bird Table Book by Tony Soper (David & Charles) gives important background information on bird feeding, including types of food which should never be offered to birds.

Who's there?

Task
Invent a simple system which will inform a person with a hearing difficulty that someone is knocking at her front door.

Age range
Nine upwards.

Group size
Small groups.

What you need
String, paper, pencils, adhesive tape, plastic-coated copper wires, batteries, bulbs, bulbholders, any other items the children may suggest.

What to do
Discuss with the children the problems of impaired hearing.

Discuss the task with them and suggest that they devise some form of visual display triggered by the knocker or bell. This could be either some sort of electronic flashing system or a mechanical device, for instance a flag or similar indicator which moves.

Well aimed!

Task
Devise a simple system for dropping a marble into a cylinder with consistent accuracy from a height of about one metre.

Age range
Seven upwards.

Group size
Small groups.

What you need
Marbles, cardboard or cardboard cylinders, staplers, scissors, adhesive, plus any other materials the children suggest.

What to do
Discuss and demonstrate the problems encountered when trying to drop a marble accurately into a cardboard tube.

   Let the children consider the problem in their groups, then devise and present solutions. Ask them to consider how this activity might be presented as a fund-raising game for a school fair.

On show

Task
Invent a means of displaying a commemorative or ornamental plate.

Age range
Nine upwards.

Group size
Pairs or individuals.

What you need
Plates, wire cutters, thin flexible wire, paper clips, cardboard, elastic bands, scissors, adhesive tape, paper plates, paints, felt-tipped pens, any other materials the children may suggest.

What to do
Discuss with the children how to display a commemorative plate or another attractive object. How can this be done so that the plate is held securely but not damaged? The children will need to decide whether their plate is to hang from a wall or be placed in some kind of stand. If they decide on the latter, how can it be made stable?

Let the children decorate paper plates and display them in the classroom using their hangers and stands.

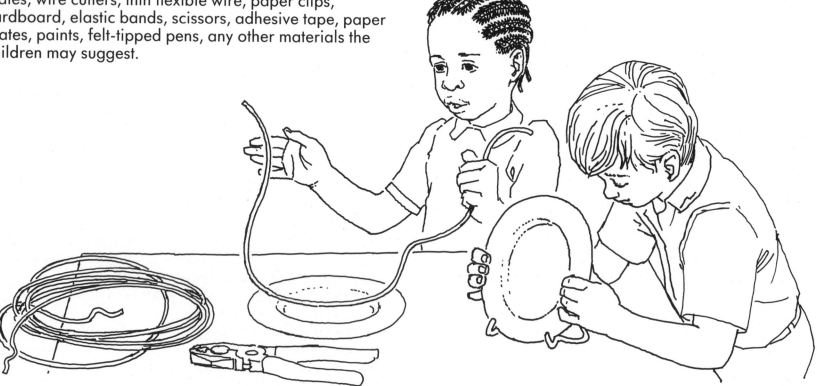

Humpty Dumpty

'Humpty Dumpty sat on a wall
Humpty Dumpty had a great fall;
All the king's horses and all the king's men
Couldn't put Humpty together again.'

Task
Invent a package to hold a raw egg so that it can be
dropped from a height of three metres without breaking.

Age range
Seven upwards.

Group size
Small groups.

What you need
Polystyrene, card, polythene, string, cotton thread, old
tights, pieces of fabric, small junk boxes, papers,
scissors, stapler, adhesive, pens, eggs.

What to do
Discuss what 'free fall' means, ie the egg cannot merely
be lowered on a string or long stick.

Tell the children that the egg can be packaged in any
way, or things can be attached to it to slow its fall, but it
must fall freely to the ground. The children also need to
think about which materials make good shock
absorbers. Do they want to decorate their packages? If
so, when should this be done?

When the children have perfected their designs, let
them write a set of instructions for others to follow. Ask
them to record those same instructions using only
pictures and symbols.

Snack bar

Task
Identify each of the seven foods in front of you without using your eyes. See photocopiable page 117.

Age range
Seven upwards.

Group size
Small groups.

What you need
Ingredients: honey, peanuts, desiccated coconut, cinnamon, apples, pears, almonds; spoons, paper plates, small dishes, knives, blindfolds, paper, pencils, copies of photocopiable page 117.

What to do
Explain to the children that they have seven foods to identify without using their eyes.

Discuss how they might go about it. Which senses will they use? Suggest that one group member should be blindfolded and should try to guess which food is which; ask another member of the group to act as recorder. These, and any other roles the children suggest, should be alternated so that all members of the group perform each role in turn. Does the task of the first child differ from that of the other children?

When each of the ingredients has been identified, ask the children to use some of them to create a lunch-time snack. Let them invent a name for the snack, then draw a diagram which shows the ingredients used to make it.

Each peach, pear, plum

Task
Explore the possible combinations of a given number of fruits.

Age range
Seven upwards.

Group size
Individuals or pairs.

What you need
Pencils, paper, crayons or coloured pens or pencils.

What to do
Read the following rhyme to the children:
'Each peach, pear, plum,
I spy Tom Thumb.'

How many different fruit drinks could Tom Thumb make using just two of the fruits? Draw the different drink mixes.

Suppose that Tom found some grapes and added these to the possible ingredients. How many different drinks could he then make? Draw the drinks. If he decided to use three ingredients, how many different drinks could he then make? Draw pictures to show all the different drinks. Make up names for each drink Tom mixed.

Action Man camouflage

Task
Design a suit for Action Man so that he is camouflaged against a jungle background from a distance of four metres.

Age range
Seven upwards.

Group size
Small groups.

What you need
Copies of photocopiable page 118, paints, crayons, pastels, coloured papers, adhesive, scissors, metre sticks or measuring tape, large sheets of paper for the background, Blu-tak or masking tape.

What to do
Give each group a copy of the Action Man outline on page 118 and ask the children to design a suit which will camouflage him against a jungle background.

Should they colour the suit or the background first? Does the order matter?

Will they allocate different tasks to different members of the group?

Matching pair

Task
Design a matching pair of gloves.

Age range
Eight upwards.

Group size
Groups of four, subdivided into pairs.

What you need
Copies of photocopiable page 119, red, yellow, blue and white paints, palettes, brushes.

What to do
Ask one pair in each group to mix colours to paint one of the gloves on photocopiable page 119 in green and purple. Remind the children that they can use only the four colours provided. Stress that they should allow the first colour time to dry before using the second.

When they have painted the glove, ask them to write instructions for the second pair to match the colours and paint the second glove.

Tropical bird

Task
Draw a pair of wings for the tropical bird on photocopiable page 120.

Age range
Seven upwards.

Group size
Individuals.

What you need
Copies of photocopiable page 120, coloured pens, crayons, pastels, paper, card, scissors.

What to do
Give the children copies of photocopiable page 120 and ask them to add a suitable pair of wings. The wings must be the same size, shape and colours. Remind them that they are looking down at the bird from above. They will need to think about how to make sure that the wings are symmetrical.

Doctor Foster's shelter

'Doctor Foster went to Gloucester
In a shower of rain.
He stepped in a puddle
Right up to his middle,
And never went there again.'

Task
Make a waterproof shelter for Doctor Foster.

Age range
Seven upwards.

Group size
Small groups.

What you need
Copies of photocopiable page 121, sheets of thin card, fabric, cardboard, wax crayons, candles, oil, food wrapping film, polythene sheeting, thin sticks, straws, adhesive, any other items the children may suggest.

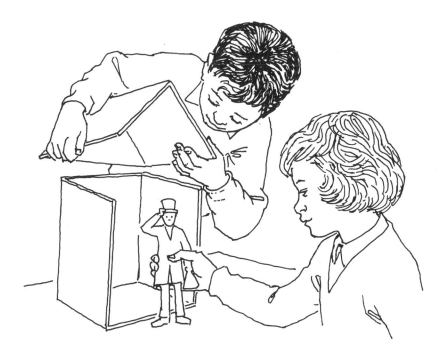

What to do
Read the rhyme to the children then present them with the photocopiable sheet. Ask them to stick the cut-out outline of Doctor Foster on to card to enable it to stand up.

Obviously, the children will need to invent a shelter which is sufficiently large to cover their figure. They may decide to make some kind of rough hut around him or alternatively devise an umbrella for him to hold. This will present the additional problem of how to attach the umbrella to the figure without it becoming unstable.

The question of waterproofing needs to be considered; some materials chosen may already have waterproof properties, others can be made waterproof. The children will also need to devise a waterproofing test. At what stage should they use the test?

Timing device

Task
Make a timing device which will tell you when ten seconds have passed.

Age range
Nine upwards.

Group size
Small groups.

What you need
Sheets of cardboard, Plasticine, marbles, funnels, empty yoghurt pots, cotton thread, seconds timer, candles, any other items the children may suggest.

What to do
Make sure the children understand what is required of a timer, then set them the task.

There are many possible solutions to this problem. Some of the most straightforward are based on rolling a marble down a slope. However, a marble will roll a fair distance in ten seconds so it is best to construct some means of slowing down the marble; for example, some kind of slalom course. Other solutions might involve: a water clock, a candle clock or even a ten second timed and taped bell or other device with a continuous sound.

Try to let the children explore possibilities as far as possible rather than steering them towards one solution.

Rain sounds

Task
Make a tape recording of three different rain sounds to accompany a poem.

Age range
Seven upwards.

Group size
Small groups.

What you need
Copies of photocopiable page 122 for each group, pencils, felt-tipped pens, tape recorders (one per group) and blank tapes, paper, tins, wood, tissue paper, other items that the children may suggest.

What to do
Read the following poem aloud to the children.

'How beautiful is the rain!
After the dust and heat,
In the broad and fiery street,
In the narrow lane,
How beautiful is the rain!

How it clatters along the roofs,
Like the tramp of hoofs!
How it gushes and struggles out
From the throat of the overflowing spout!

Across the window-pane
It pours and pours;
And swift and wide,
With a muddy tide,
Like a river down the gutter roars,
The rain, the welcome rain!'

H W Longfellow

Give each group copies of photocopiable page 122. Let the children decorate them appropriately.

Ask the children to make up and record three different rain sounds to accompany the poem. Can the rest of the class identify the sounds?

Display the decorated poems and let the children devise a class assembly around the poem and their recordings.

Bonfire Night sounds

Task
Make a tape recording to represent Bonfire Night. It should last about two minutes.

Age range
Seven upwards.

Group size
Small groups.

What you need
A tape recorder and blank tape for each group, sandpaper, dried peas, rice, coffee beans, a drum, maracas, tissue paper, bells, a cymbal, a bottle with a lid, any other items the children might suggest.

What to do
Present the task to the children. You will need to decide whether it is possible to have more than one group working on the problem at a time.

The children can use any of the items provided or any others you can find in the room. Do not let them forget to use their own voices!

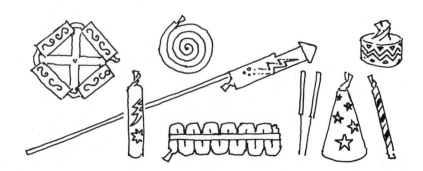

TV advertisement

Task
Make up a television advertisement encouraging people to use lead-free petrol. It should last about half a minute.

Age range
Seven upwards.

Group size
Small groups.

What you need
Paper, pencils, timers, tape recorders and blank tapes.

What to do
Explain to the children why it is preferable to use lead-free petrol. Do they need to do any research about this first?

They will also need to think about any props which might help to put across their message to the audience.

Let them act out their advertisements to another group, then ask them to swap scripts and act out the other group's advertisement. Can they suggest any improvements?

Radio commercial

Task
Make a radio commercial asking people to save their aluminium cans in aid of a conservation organisation. The advertisement should last approximately one minute.

Age range
Eight upwards.

Group size
Small groups.

What you need
Paper, pencils, timers, tape recorders and blank tapes.

What to do
Discuss with the children the benefits of recycling waste.

The children will need to think about what information should be included in their commercial; for instance they should give details of what is to be done with the cans. Should they also include a test to identify which cans are made from aluminium?

Play the advertisements to the rest of the school in assembly.

What's the question?

Task
Formulate three questions, the solutions to which are to be found on photocopiable page 123.

Age range
Eight upwards.

Group size
Individuals or pairs.

What you need
Copies of photocopiable page 123, pencils, paper, clip boards.

What to do
Present the children with the photocopiable sheet. Discuss with them what is required. Explain that each question will probably consist of several sentences and should provide all the information needed for someone to work out the problem. Avoid questions which pose simple problems of computation.

Let the children test their questions on children in another class.

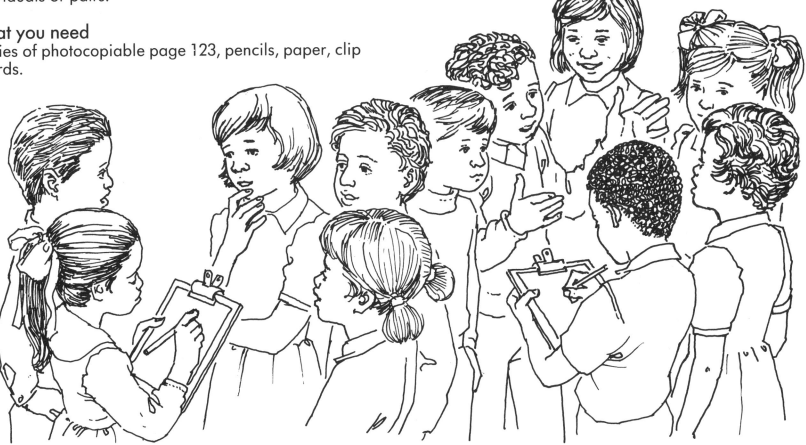

Tea party

Task
Make invitations, place settings and menus for a 'Mad Hatter's tea party'.

Age range
Nine upwards.

Group size
Small groups.

What you need
A copy of Lewis Carroll's *Alice in Wonderland*, paper, coloured and white cardboard sheets, coloured pens, adhesive, scissors.

What to do
Read to the children the chapter in *Alice in Wonderland* about the Mad Hatter's tea party.

Ask them to produce invitations, place settings and menus for a 'Mad Hatter's tea party' for the four characters they would most like to meet.

There are various ways the children might approach this problem. They may allocate specific tasks such as 'all the menus' to one member of the group; but they will need to agree on their guest list before embarking on the separate parts of the problem.

Follow-up
Devise a pop party or a football party, or any other party with a specific theme. Ask the children who they would like to invite and to construct an appropriate menu for the party.

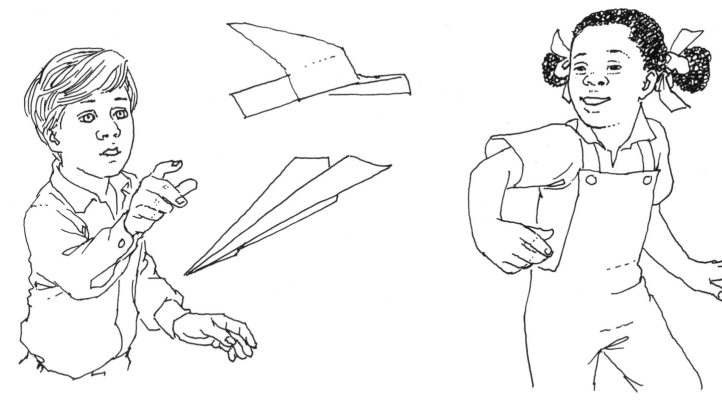

Paper aeroplane

Task
Design and make a paper aeroplane.

Age range
Seven upwards.

Group size
Small groups or individuals.

What you need
A4-size paper (an old telephone directory is a useful source), scissors, adhesive.

What to do
Present the task to the children. They will need to experiment with various forms of design before refining a particular model.

How can they ensure that their testing of models is fair. Where will the testing take place? Which aeroplane flies the farthest? Why?

Follow-up
Set the task of making an aeroplane that must be launched from a predetermined spot and land in a defined area three metres away.

Instructions

Task
Produce a set of written instructions for a specific task and translate them into pictorial form.

Age range
Nine upwards.

Group size
Small groups.

What you need
Drawing materials, paper.

What to do
Divide the groups into two sets. Set one has to devise a set of written instructions to enable someone to carry out a simple task, for instance cleaning a pair of shoes. The other set has to translate these written instructions into pictorial form.

The children will have to break down the task into separate stages and think about the order and sequence of the operation.

Can the children represent the instructions as a flow chart?

Containers

Task
Design and make a container with a lid, from one sheet of A4-size card, which will hold the greatest volume of sand.

Age range
Nine upwards.

Group size
Small groups.

What you need
Sheets of thin A4-size card, rulers, pencils, fine sand, adhesive, paper clips, scissors, staplers, adhesive tape.

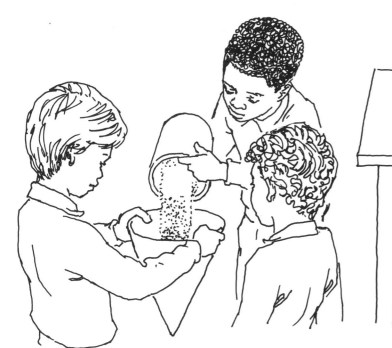

What to do
You may wish to present the problem as it stands, or you may prefer to discuss the various possible shapes of container, for example cube, cuboid, cylinder, pyramid etc.

How will the children measure the sand? They need to establish this to ensure fair testing of their containers.

Tiddly-winks target

Task
Devise and make a simple piece of equipment which will project a draughts piece into a small container such as a mug from a distance of about 60 cm.

Age range
Nine upwards.

Group size
Small groups.

What you need
Paper, drawing materials, draughts pieces, old mugs, adhesives, elastic bands, any other items the children may suggest.

What to do
Encourage the children to think about a range of ideas and sketch them before embarking on the production of a working model. If they find it easier, let them form smaller groups, or pairs, and try out various ideas. They can then come back together into their original groupings to test which is the most effective idea.

3D greetings card

Task
Design and make a three-dimensional greetings card for a specific occasion using only one sheet of A4-size card.

Age range
Nine upwards.

Group size
Individuals or pairs.

What you need
Thin sheets of A4-size card, scissors, craft knives, rulers, drawing materials.

What to do
Discuss with the children the variety of events for which greetings cards are sent.

Ask them to produce their own three-dimensional greetings card using only one sheet of A4 card. The three-dimensional quality must be obtained only by cutting and folding. The card must fold flat to fit into an envelope. Ask the children to decorate the cards.

When the cards are completed, ask the children to write an accompanying set of instructions with no more than five stages on how they were made.

Gozunder

Task
Design and make a simple system which will retrieve small objects which have fallen under chairs, settees, beds etc without the user having to bend down to pick them up.

Age range
Nine upwards.

Group size
Small groups.

What you need
Paper, pencils, wood, hack-saws, hammers, nails, elastic bands, adhesive tape, PVA adhesive, mirrors.

What to do
Discuss the problem of retrieving items which have disappeared under furniture. This could be particularly difficult for the elderly or for those with back problems. Some items would be out of sight, so the retrieval system would need to include a means of seeing the object without the person having to fumble around on hands and knees, as well as a device for retrieving it.

Holiday dream

Task
Create an imaginary holiday area which will attract people by the facilities it offers, then produce a holiday brochure for the resort.

Age range
Nine upwards.

Group size
Whole class, small groups.

What you need
Paper, pencils, pens, crayons, staplers.

What to do
Discuss with the children what they would do if they suddenly found they owned a large plot of land 'away from it all'. They then have to suggest how best to develop it as a holiday resort and what they would put there to attract holidaymakers.

This problem could be tackled initially by a class brainstorming session and then small groups could be established, each with a different task such as transport management, entertainment and sporting activities, catering, accommodation etc. Each group could be asked to submit a report to an editorial committee, whose responsibility would be to collaborate with all the groups to plan, write and illustrate the booklet.

It should be a rule that the preservation of the environment has to guide all decisions made. Bearing this in mind, the children could also elect a 'green' committee.

Chair toy

Task
Create a child's toy by converting an ordinary classroom chair.

Age range
Nine upwards.

Group size
Small groups.

What you need
As many classroom chairs as you have groups, card, newspaper, large sheets of paper, paint, wood, string, elastic bands, adhesive tape, any other items the children may suggest.

What to do
Discuss with the class how young children often find pleasure in simple playthings which allow for imaginative freedom, for example a large cardboard box which can become anything the young child wishes.

Ask the children to use the chair as the base for creating an imaginative toy which can be enjoyed by younger children. They should have a target age-group in mind before embarking on the construction of the toy. The finished toy could be tested in the nursery or infant school, after which any necessary modifications could be made.

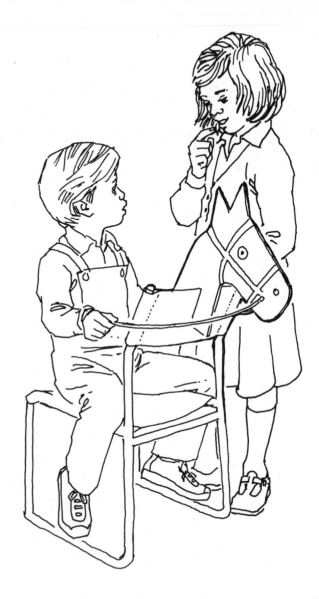

Fruit picker

Task
Design and make a device for picking apples from the highest parts of the tree without having to climb the tree.

Age range
Eight upwards.

Group size
Small groups.

What you need
Paper, pencils, hammers, wood, hack-saws, elastic bands, adhesives, netting, fabric, flexible wire, string, wire coat-hangers, tubes (card or plastic), measuring tapes.

What to do
Discuss how difficult it is and the danger involved when picking fruit from the highest branches of an apple tree.

Then ask the children to design and make a piece of equipment long enough to reach the top of an apple tree, which will cut off the fruit without damaging it and contain it so that it does not fall to the ground and bruise.

How will they work out the length needed to reach the top of the tree? Obviously, they will need to do this before starting to make the device.

Improvise

Task
Devise and present an 'improvisation kit' for use in case of emergencies.

Age range
Nine upwards.

Group size
Small groups.

What you need
Paper, pencils, felt-tipped pens, scrap materials, adhesive, scissors, string, adhesive tape.

What to do
Discuss with the children how most people have at some time experienced the problem of having to 'make do' when something has broken or is unavailable. For example, we tuck our trousers into our socks if we do not have bicycle clips; if no display cabinet is available we use an empty ice-cream container to house a precious collection of items.

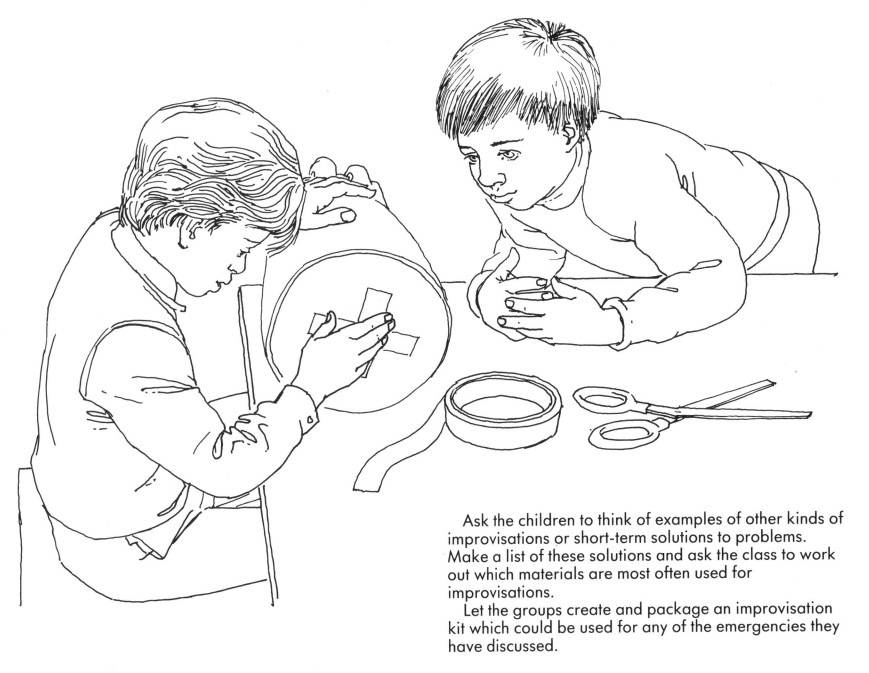

Ask the children to think of examples of other kinds of improvisations or short-term solutions to problems. Make a list of these solutions and ask the class to work out which materials are most often used for improvisations.

Let the groups create and package an improvisation kit which could be used for any of the emergencies they have discussed.

Make a maze

Task
Design a maze.

Age range
Seven upwards.

Group size
Small groups.

What you need
Paper, pencils, felt-tipped pens, card, scissors, adhesive.

What to do
Discuss with the class the origins and purposes of the maze. Can they think of any examples of mazes in stories? Have any of the children ever seen a maze, for

example a maze in a garden? Many of the children will also be familiar with mazes through comics and puzzle books.

After discussion, ask the children to devise and draw a maze of their own and try it out on their friends.

Older children will be capable of devising quite sophisticated mazes containing complex routes. This could be further developed by asking them to construct mazes from card and from this devise games containing penalty and plus points.

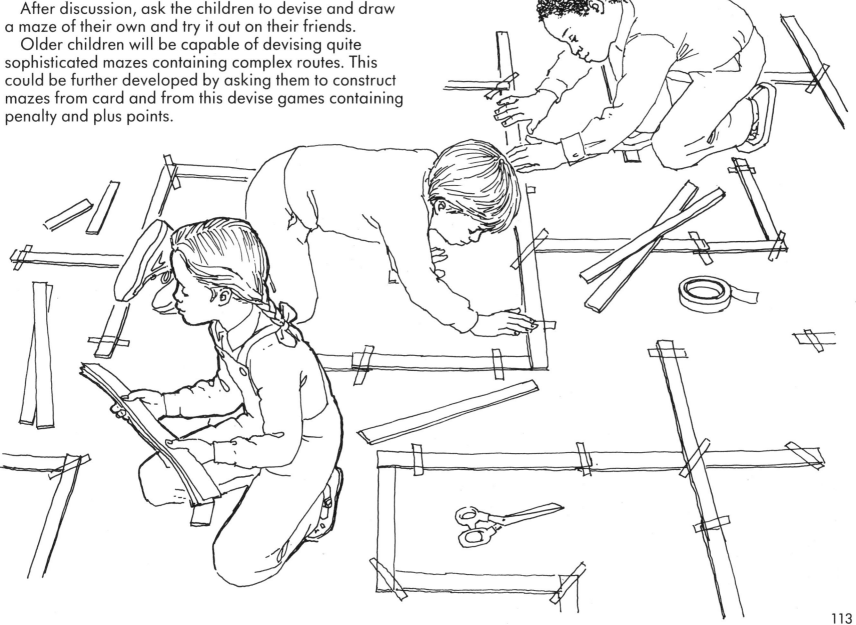

How often?

Task
Discover and record the frequency with which letters are used in a paragraph of text. Record the findings and compare them with those of other groups.

Age range
Nine upwards.

Group size
Small groups.

What you need
Pieces of text of equal length (appropriate to the children's ages and abilities), squared paper, newspapers, magazines, pencils.

What to do
Discuss with the children how although the alphabet contains only 26 letters, books and newspapers contain thousands of different words. Obviously these 26 letters are used many times, but are some used more often than others?

Ask groups of children to examine their pieces of text and choose a way of recording the frequency with which letters occur. Once they have recorded the number of times each letter is used, ask them to put them in order of highest or lowest frequency.

Follow-up

More able children could be asked to work out the frequency with which vowels are used in the text and to express this as a fraction or percentage.

A further examination of text could reveal the letters which are most often used to begin or end words.

Reproducible material

Snack bar, see page 88

Fill in the chart for each child, saying whether or not their guess was correct.

	NAME	HONEY	PEANUTS	DESICCATED COCONUT	CINNAMON	APPLES	PEARS	ALMONDS
1								
2								
3								
4								
5								
6								
7								
8								
9								
10								

Action Man camouflage, see page 90

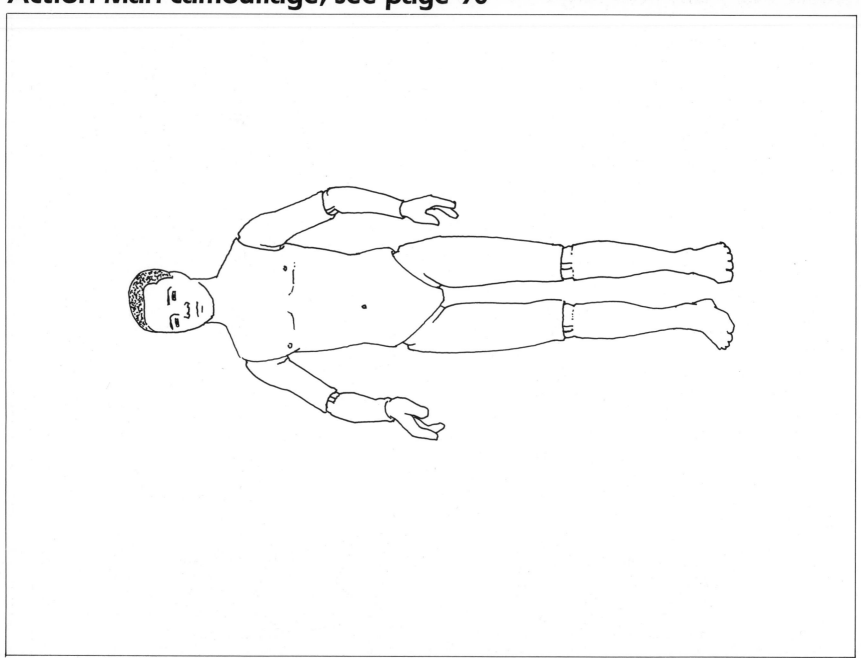

Matching pair, see page 91

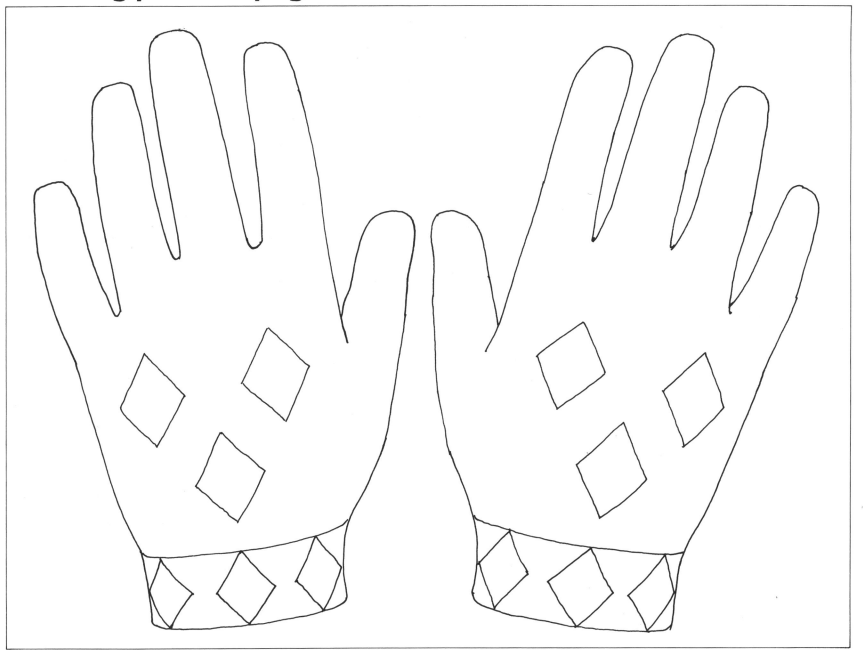

Tropical bird, see page 92

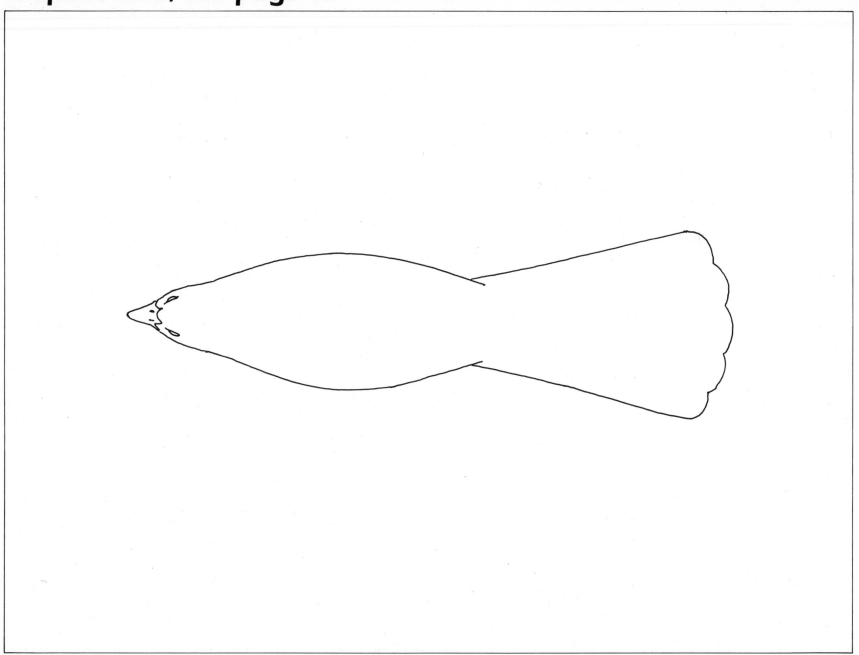

Doctor Foster's shelter, see page 93

Rain sounds, see page 95

'How beautiful is the rain!
After the dust and heat,
In the broad and fiery street,
In the narrow lane,
How beautiful is the rain!

How it clatters along the roofs,
Like the tramp of hoofs!
How it gushes and struggles out
From the throat of the overflowing spout!

Across the window-pane
It pours and pours;
And swift and wide,
With a muddy tide,
Like a river down the gutter roars,
The rain, the welcome rain!'

H W Longfellow

What's the question? see page 99

Here are three answers: 37p, 37cm, 37 buses. Invent three questions which give these answers and test them out on your friends. Note down the questions they think up.

1

2

3

This page may be photocopied for use in the classroom and should not be declared in any return in respect of any photocopying licence.

Resources

It is best to try to collect together in advance a good range of resources for your 'problem-solving environment'. These can range from the scrap materials found in every classroom to more specialised technical equipment.

Scrap materials
These should include basic items such as the following:
cotton reels
pipe-cleaners
cardboard boxes in a variety of shapes and sizes
inner tubes from toilet rolls
ice-cream tubs
yoghurt pots
margarine tubs
foam offcuts
corks
bottle tops
empty film cannisters
old felt-tipped or ball-point pen barrels
wire coat-hangers
coffe jar lids
jam jars
scraps of fabric
ice lolly sticks
wood offcuts.

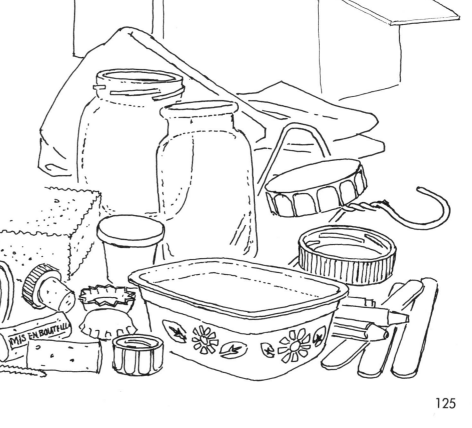

Craft, design and technology materials

The more art and craft materials the better, but a basic list should include:

art straws
beads
polystyrene spheres
sponges
Blu-tack
drawing pins
elastic bands
PVA adhesive
latex adhesive
glue guns and sticks*
hole punch
paper clips
paper-fasteners
stapler
string
adhesive tape
masking tape
bulldog clips
wire
wire twists
dowelling
wooden wheels
pencils
felt-tipped pens
crayons
erasers
inks
paints
brushes
mixing palettes
rulers
hack-saws
bench-hooks

drill*
scissors
screwdriver*
sandpaper
vice
craft knife*
wire cutters
safety rule
saw
hammer
pliers
file
batteries
battery holders
bulbs and holders
crocodile clips
plastic-coated copper wire.

*Use of these items should be carefully supervised.

Paper and card

A good supply of different types of paper and card in all colours and sizes is essential. This should include:

cardboard pieces
corrugated card
Corriflute
newspaper
sugar paper
cartridge paper
lined and squared paper
tissue paper
gift wrapping paper
tin foil
waxed paper

Miscellaneous

The following items will also prove useful:
interlocking cubes
marbles
balloons
Plasticine
plastic tubing
tape recorder
timers
dice
Kits such as LEGO, LEGO Technic and Quadro.

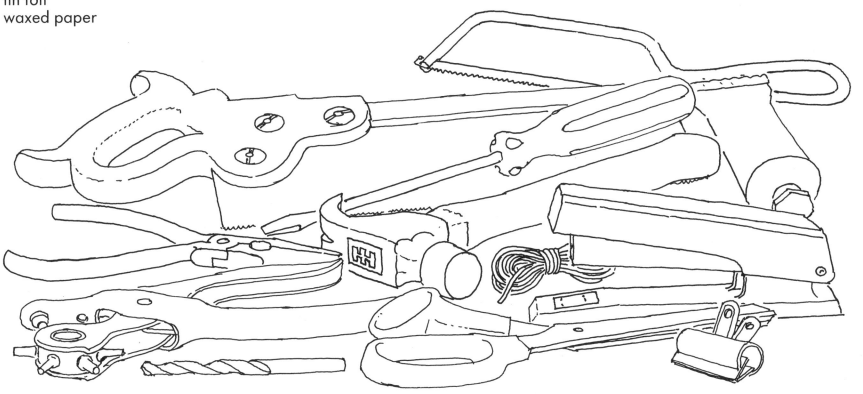

Other Scholastic books

Bright Ideas
The *Bright Ideas* books provide a wealth of resources for busy primary school teachers. There are now more than 20 titles published, providing clearly explained and illustrated ideas on topics ranging from *Spelling* and *Maths Games* to *World of Work* and *Using Books in the Classroom*. Each book contains material which can be photocopied for use in the classroom.

Teacher Handbooks
The *Teacher Handbooks* give an overview of the latest research in primary education, and show how it can be put into practice in the classroom. Covering all the core areas of the curriculum, the *Teacher Handbooks* are indispensable to the new teacher as a source of information and useful to the experienced teacher as a quick reference guide.

Management Books
The *Management Books* are designed to help teachers to organise their time, classroom and teaching more efficiently. The books deal with topical issues, such as *Parents and Schools* and organising and planning *Project Teaching*, and are written by authors with lots of practical advice and experiences to share.

Let's Investigate
Let's Investigate is an exciting range of photocopiable activity books giving open-ended investigative tasks. Designed to cover the 6 to 12-year-old age range these books are ideal for small group or individual work. Each book presents progressively more difficult concepts and many of the activities can be adapted for use throughout the primary school. Detailed teacher's notes outlining the objectives of each photocopiable sheet and suggesting follow-up activities have been included.